The Countryside Cartoon Joke Book

Roger Penwill

Merlin Unwin Books

First published by Merlin Unwin Books, 2008

Published by:
Merlin Unwin Books
Palmers House, 7 Corve Street
Ludlow, Shropshire SY8 1DB (U.K.)
www.merlinunwin.co.uk

British Library Cataloguing-in-Publication Data:
A catalogue record for this book is available from the British Library.
The author asserts his right to be identified with this work.

ISBN 978 1 906122 05 8

Designed and typeset by Merlin Unwin Books, Ludlow.
Printed by Leo Paper Products.

Foreword

Not many of us have much of a say where we are born and after that where are brought up. If I had any say at all I don't think I could have said it very well as I was born a townie; just missed being a cockney, in fact. If the wind had been in a different direction I certainly would have been. When I was seven we moved to the eastern end of the District Line and were near the edge of civilisation as this almost-a-cockney knew it... almost the countryside.

When we moved, my father bought his first car. Back then people went out for afternoon drives just for the pleasure of it and in doing so invented the Sunday driver. My first experiences beyond the far end of the District Line into proper countryside were the villages, commons and pubs of south Essex. R. Whites ginger beer and real crisps with blue bags of damp salt. Holidays on farms in Cornwall: seeing a calf born; riding a tractor.

Having worked in London and lived in its suburbia for years, it was a great relief to discover that this almost-a-cockney exterior of mine contained a countryman eager to get out. Well, he's now well out and living in Olde England on the Herefordshire/Shropshire border. It's a joy to live in a friendly, caring community. You can say hello to strangers without them ignoring you, regarding you as some form of nutter or giving you a thump.

It's modern communications that allow me to be a cartoonist in the countryside. Thanks to email and the internet I can conduct my business anywhere. There are a growing number of us homeworking types, which has to be good news for the countryside. Dormitory villages are becoming less sleepy, with some newcomers around during the day, pretending they've lived there for years.

As Joni Mitchell might have put it, I've looked at life from both sides now; well, town and country life anyway. Some of the cartoons in this book appeared first in *The Countryman* magazine, some have been published by *Country Cards* and the rest are new. I hope you enjoy this countryside Johnny-Come-Lately's view of the world around him.

Roger Penwill, April 2008

The cartoonist

Roger Penwill is the founder of the Shrewsbury Cartoon Festival and co-founder of the Professional Cartoonists Organisation. He is a past President of the international Federation of Cartoonists Organisations and is a Fellow of the Royal Society of Arts.

He is married with a daughter and son and lives in the village of Brimfield in north Herefordshire.

To Erin and Amelia

"THIS WAY I STILL HOLD UP TRAFFIC
BUT THEY DON'T SEEM TO MIND"

"I HEAR GILES HAS CONVERTED TO GAS"

"THIS TIME HE'S OBJECTING TO OUR WIND FARM"

"AFTER A WHILE YOU'LL ADAPT TO
THE WIND AROUND THESE PARTS"

"IT'S TAKEN A WHILE, BUT WE ARE NOW SELF-SUFFICIENT,
– ALTHOUGH ONLY IN HATS"

FELL WALKING

Community Hospital

Accident and Emergency

"AMAZING VIEW UP HERE. ON A CLEAR DAY
YOU CAN SEE YOUR FEET"

"YOU WON'T GET ME BELIEVING THE SCARE STORIES
ABOUT THE EFFECTS OF G.M. CROPS"

"CHARLES BELIEVES ADAPTING TO COUNTRY LIFE IS A GRADUAL PROCESS"

"WITH THIS MAP YOU ALWAYS KNOW
EXACTLY WHERE YOU ARE"

TEA
TENT

PENWILL

"THE SIGN IS UTTER NONSENSE, SIR –
THEY STOPPED LAYING A WEEK AGO"

"DON'T WORRY – I WOULDN'T SELL TO SOMEONE WHO MIGHT DESTROY THE CHARACTER OF THE PROPERTY"

"YOU WON'T GET SMELLS LIKE THIS
ON THE INTERNET"

"THAT'S HIM!"

"AND YOU'D NEVER GUESS THAT THIS NEW
OFFICE FACILITY WAS ONCE THE OLD STY"

"IF YOU'RE THERE FOR YESTERDAY'S BUS
YOU'VE JUST MISSED IT"

"HURRY, THE ALARM'S GONE OFF — THE POLICE
WILL BE HERE IN THREE HOURS!"

"I KNOW MY HUSBAND WAS YOUR YOUNGEST AND
WEAKEST CHILD BUT YOU MUST STOP PUTTING
HIM IN THE AGA."

"PSST! – WANT TO SEE SOME REAL ENGLISH APPLES?"

35

"NOTHING BEATS TOAST MADE BY AN OPEN FIRE"

"WELL AT LEAST ONE GOVERNMENT MP NOW KNOWS WHERE MILK COMES FROM"

"OH DEAR... THE MAJOR'S COME ON THE SHOOT AGAIN"

" IT SAYS HERE THE BEACH RESTORATION WILL ALSO REMOVE UNSIGHTLY RELICS OF THE PAST "

"CLIVE STILL LIKES TO DRESS FOR THE OFFICE EACH DAY"

43

44

45

"IT'S NOT WORTH SELLING THE WOOL SO WE MAKE PULLOVERS TO KEEP THE SHEEP WARM AFTER SHEARING"

"I CONSIDERED DIVERSIFYING INTO OSTRICHES
BUT THEY'RE THE DEVIL TO SHEAR"

"COME BOYS - THERE HAS TO BE SOMETHING YOU'VE LEARNT ABOUT WOODLAND HABITAT OTHER THAN THERE'S NO DECENT SURFACES FOR GRAFFITTI"

"WE'RE FINE THROUGH HERE - THIS IS A BRIDAL WAY"

"JUST BECAUSE IT'S A BIT ROUGH, YOU'RE NOT
HAVING ANOTHER DAY OFF SCHOOL"

"HE'S THE LAST ONE. HOW WILL I GET TO
SLEEP JUST COUNTING HIM?"

" DO FIVE BEANS AND A COURGETTE COUNT AS
BEING SELF·SUFFICIENT ? "

"THIS IS THE LAST AVAILABLE"

"SOMEHOW HANGING A PHOTO IS NOT SO ROMANTIC
AS THE REAL THING"

"NO, YOU CAN'T KNOCK DOWN YOUR SANDCASTLE
- IT'S JUST BEEN GRADE 2 LISTED"

"THIS IS MY NEW HERD — COUNTRY CRAFTS"

"SIMON HAS TO BE READY AT A MOMENT'S NOTICE"

"TO BE HONEST HAROLD, I DON'T THINK THAT WILL STOP THE EROSION"

"DID I MENTION THAT DARREN'S A PART-TIME FIREFIGHTER?"

"WE HAD THEM FOOLED UNTIL YOU ASKED
THEM TO HURRY UP BECAUSE WE
HAD TO GET BACK TO LONDON"

"THEN ONCE YOU GET SAM OUT YOU'LL HAVE TO GET THE THREE SHEEP AND THE DOG HE WENT IN AFTER"

"MOVE ALONG SONNY- WE'VE A CONTRACT TO
GIVE THIS TREE PROTECTION"

"HE'S THE SORT OF BOUNDER THAT GIVES OUR SPORT A BAD IMAGE"

"NO - DON'T GO IN THERE - IT'S FRIGHTFUL
- IT'S JUST SO UNTIDY !"

"SORRY – THIS IS FOR EXPORT – YOU'LL HAVE TO BUY IMPORTED STUFF AT THE GARDEN CENTRE"

"I'M FINE, MISS, BUT ROSIE HERE'S NOT FEELING TOO CLEVER"

"THIS IS THE LAST TIME WE IMPORT OUR
CHRISTMAS HOLLY FROM JAPAN"

"IT'S IMPORTED EACH MONTH FROM POLAND"

"STOP THAT OPERATION AT ONCE! – THAT MAN
HAS NO LICENCE TO SING"

" AT LAST I'VE CONVINCED HIM TO SEE A DOCTOR"

"RE-INTRODUCING THE LYNX INTO THE WILD
– WHATEVER NEXT?"

"DO YOU THINK I SHOULD ADVISE HIM
AGAINST CYCLING FURTHER TODAY?"

"THERE'S ONE!"

" SHE SAID SHE COULDN'T ABIDE SOME TYPES OF HOLLY.
I SAID 'WHICH?' THEN SHE HIT ME "

" WE'VE COOKED OUR SAUSAGES – NOW CAN WE HAVE OUR BAPS AND KETCHUP? "

"AT LEAST WITH GLOBAL WARMING WE DON'T **HAVE THE** BAD WINTERS WE USED TO"

"THE KITCHEN'S IN THE NEXT VILLAGE"

"I'VE TOLD YOU BEFORE ABOUT GOING OUT ON A NIGHT LIKE THIS"

"I THOUGHT THE GOVERNMENT ENCOURAGED WIND FARMS"

"I REMEMBER IT WELL. BAGGED LOADS
OF THE BLIGHTERS"

"MIRANDA LIKES TO SERVE HER NETTLE TEA FRESH"

"IT'S GOOD NOW...SO IMAGINE HOW SPLENDID A COUNTRY BUS SERVICE THIS'LL BE IN SIXTY YEARS' TIME"

PENWILL

"OLD SHEP'S TEACHING THE NEW DOG HIS SPECIAL METHOD"

" THAT ONE "

"OLD WILL SAYS COULD WE SPEAK UP A BIT SO HE CAN ACCIDENTALLY OVERHEAR US"

"WEREN'T WE FOLLOWING THE ONE-HOUR CIRCULAR YELLOW ROUTE?"

"THERE COULD BE TROUBLE TONIGHT..."

"THE NOTE SAYS 'NO NUTS TOMORROW THANK YOU'"

" IT'S NOT FAIR- JUST BECAUSE THEY LIKE
HIS CHOICE OF MUSIC THEY GET FED"

"STOP COMPLAINING, MOTHER – FRESH AIR WILL DO YOU GOOD "

"GEMMA ONLY AGREED TO BE MY VALENTINE
IF WE SHARED A WATERBUTT"

" THEY'RE HARES, LAD — YOU CAN'T EXPECT
THEM TO STICK TO QUEENSBURY RULES "

"THE WORST THING IS THE PRESS INTRUSION"

"NO, MY DEARS, THIS BE SUMMER... YOU'VE MISSED
SPRING ... FEBRUARY 17TH THAT WAS "

MODERN TECHNOLOGY ALLOWED KEVIN TO WORK FROM
HOME AND ENJOY LIVING IN THE HEART OF THE COUNTRY

"WELL, THE MAP REFERENCE MUST BE WRONG"

"NATURE HAS ERODED THESE ROCKS INTO SHAPES
THAT ARE JUST OUT OF THIS WORLD"

"MUST BE AN ANCIENT WAYMARKER"

"WE WON'T GET LOST. I'M LINKED TO A GLOBAL
POSITIONING SYSTEM USING LOW ORBIT SATELLITES"

115

" PERHAPS IT DOESN'T APPLY TO BACON"

"SOMEHOW, A CYCLE PATH CROSSES THE
CANAL JUST ABOUT HERE"

119

"I HOPE YOU CAN CAPTURE THE FROTHY CLOUDS"

COUNTRY ROAD RAGE

"IT DOES SAY 'STICK TO FOOTPATHS'"

Other humour books from Merlin Unwin

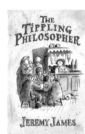